MY FASHION ADDICTION

Coloring Book 10 Year Old Girl

EDUCANDO
KIDS

Let's color these fashionable Girls!

Enjoy!

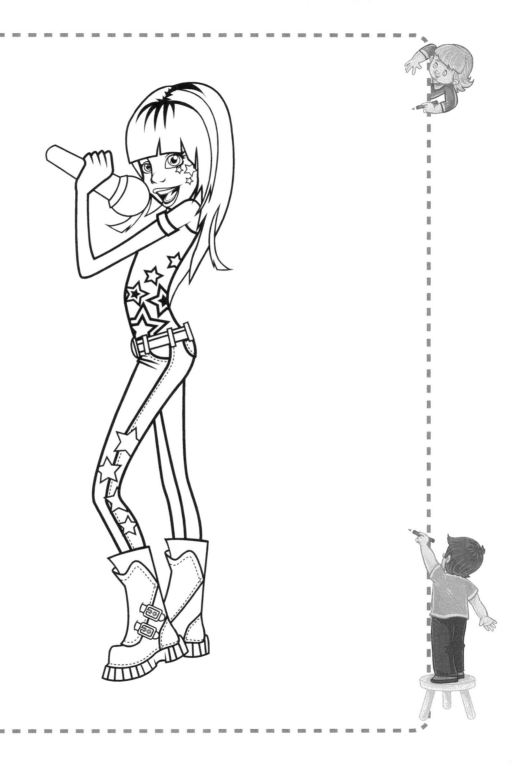

This is a Bleed Through Page If You Are Using a Coloring Marker or Pen!
Find Other Great Titles By searching for Educando Kids on Your Favorite Book Retailer
Amazon.Com | Barnes & Noble (BN.Com) | Books A Million (BAM.Com)

EDUCANDO
KIDS

CPSIA information can be obtained
at www.ICGtesting.com
Printed in the USA
BVHW020224051222
653465BV00010B/437